LEGO NEXO KNIGHTS

NEXO POWER

NEXO KNIGHTS™
HANDBOOK

By Tracey West

Scholastic Children's Books
Euston House,
24 Eversholt Street,
London NW1 1DB, UK

A division of Scholastic Ltd
Mexico City ~ New Delhi ~ Hong Kong
London ~ New York ~ Toronto ~ Sydney ~ Auckland

This book was first published in the US ~~~~~~~~~~~ LLC.
Published in t~~~~~~~~~~~~~

FSC
www.fsc.org
MIX
Paper from

Our Story Begins . . .

. . . in the kingdom of Knighton, a land where knights and robots live side by side. A land where magic and technology work together to keep the kingdom running smoothly. When things don't run smoothly, knights are always there to lend a helping sword. Most kids in Knighton grow up wanting to become knights.

For Clay Moorington, Lance Richmond, Aaron Fox, Macy Halbert and Axl, that dream came true when they graduated from the Knights' Academy. The new knights were given powerful shields in front of the entire kingdom, and they were deemed Knights of Future Technology. But while the happy villagers cheered their favourite heroes in shining armour, there was trouble brewing in Knighton.

The Book of Monsters

The Book of Monsters was alive. It could talk, think and plan. Within its pages lurked all of the most fearsome monsters the world had ever seen. To protect Knighton, the book was safely locked in the library of Merlok, the king's wizard, but it waited patiently to one day be free again . . .

Finally, the book found the perfect puppet for its plans in Jestro, the court jester. Jestro had no friends in the kingdom except for Clay Moorington. Clay tried to be kind to the jester, but everyone else thought Jestro was a joke – and not the funny kind. Jestro was tired of everyone laughing at him instead of with him.

Lonely and eager to prove that he was nothing to be laughed at, Jestro was a perfect target for The Book of Monsters' offer. If Jestro freed it, together they could unleash an evil on Knighton. Soon, the citizens of Knighton would be serving Jestro, not laughing at him

Merlok's Sacrifice

Jestro and The Book of Monsters launched their attack right away. With a wave of a magic staff over the pages of The Book of Monsters, evil monsters sprung to life. The knights bravely fought them, but muscle and iron are no match against magic monsters. Only one man could take them down.

Enter Merlok, the amazing wizard. He cast a massive magic spell to stop the monsters and . . . *boom!* Jestro and The Book of Monsters were blown far away from the castle. Although the monsters were defeated, Merlok's library was destroyed, and dangerous Books of Evil had been scattered across the kingdom. Worst of all, Merlok was gone.

The NEXO KNIGHTS Team

Even though Merlok had disappeared, he wasn't gone forever! The wizard had managed to save a copy of himself inside the Knighton computer network. Now he's able to harness the power of magic and technology together. In his new form, Merlok 2.0 can download magical NEXO Powers to the knights, so they can defeat whatever monsters attack.

Now it's a fair fight. Clay, Lance, Aaron, Axl and Macy train with their NEXO Weapons and NEXO Shields so they'll always be ready when Jestro and The Book of Monsters attack – and they will! The knights have only just begun to see what Jestro's monsters can do . . .

NEXO KNIGHTS Heroes

Who do you call when monsters attack? The NEXO KNIGHTS team! They'll race to the scene and fight off the bad guys with their NEXO Weapons.

And who are these knights? Clay, Lance, Aaron, Axl and Macy have just graduated from the Knights' Academy. None of them are as polished as Lance's armour yet, but each one of them is determined to keep Knighton safe, no matter what it takes.

But the knights can't do it alone. They've got Merlok 2.0 to download NEXO Powers to their shields and weapons. Young knights-in-training Robin Underwood and Ava Prentis lend their tech skills to keep all their equipment in top shape. King and Queen Halbert are always there to cheer them on. And for everything else that needs to get done, there's a small army of Squirebots.

CLAY MOORINGTON

To Clay, being a knight is serious business, so he takes his training very, very seriously. He watches training films for fun, he has memorized the entire Knights' Code, and he spends more time practising his moves than sleeping. Clay loves to come up with stuff like training schedules and battle plans for the other knights.

That means that Clay can be bossy, but he backs it up with solid fighting skills and nerves as strong as the metal in his sword. When you're in trouble and need a hero, Clay is the guy you want to show up.

Monsters don't scare Clay – but lazy teammates do. That's why he and Lance are constantly butting their helmeted heads!

KNIGHT KNOTES

- ▶ Clay is an orphan from the small farming village of Dnullib.
- ▶ Clay has been called "The Knight's Knight".
- ▶ Good-guy Clay and evil Jestro were once friends.

"I am the only one who truly lives by the Knights' Code!"

LANCE RICHMOND

You need to put on your sunglasses when you see Lance, because his armour is so super shiny! He didn't polish it himself, though – it was probably one of his many Squirebot servants, or maybe even Dennis, his own personal Squirebot butler.

Lance would rather spend the night at a knight club than spend it doing knight training. His money buys him the coolest outfits and most expensive weapons. He's witty, charming, good-looking – and popular with everyone except Clay, who wishes Lance would take training more seriously.

Lance might be a spoiled party boy, but a hero's heart beats somewhere underneath all that shiny armour. He's going to need to tap into his hero side once the evil monsters start attacking the kingdom!

KNIGHT KNOTES

► Lance's dad is a wealthy lord.

► He hates to miss his midday massage.

► Lance has been known to pay someone to finish a fight for him if he feels like he's getting too sweaty.

"Relaxation is an important part of my training regimen. The only part, really."

AARON FOX

**"This is pretty awesome.
Like, awesome-awesome."**

Trouble ahead? Monsters attacking? People in danger? That's all Aaron needs to hear before he rushes off to save the day – totally without thinking. But who needs a plan when you've got enough adrenaline running through you to power the whole kingdom?

Aaron is a thrill seeker who rides his shield like a hoverboard, looking for waves to surf and mountains to climb. Clay thinks he's irresponsible, but Aaron's fans love his "mad skillz".

Those skillz – um, skills – come in handy when Jestro and The Book of Monsters attack Knighton. Aaron will do anything to save his kingdom. He's just got to be careful that his daredevil ways won't get him into trouble.

KNIGHT KNOTES

► Aaron likes to chill as much as he likes thrills – mostly by playing video games and watching TV.

► He grew up near the beach, in the fishing village of Grindstead.

► Aaron is into "Knightkour", which means he uses all of Knighton like a big obstacle course by running, jumping and climbing over anything in his path.

AXL

This gentle giant is always hungry for action – and for dinner! That's pretty much all Axl thinks about, but hey, it takes a lot of food to keep a guy his size going.

Axl is the biggest and most physically powerful of the knights. He's basically a sweetheart, but if you get him angry, watch out! He'll mash you like a potato and then go and eat some mashed potatoes, because mashing you made him hungry.

Born into a family of giants, Axl still grew up to be the largest one in his family (and anybody's family!). He worked out at a young age by moving rocks in his mountain mining town of Digginton. Axl will soon learn that he'll need more than brute strength to defeat Jestro's monsters – he'll need magic, too.

KNIGHT KNOTES

▶ Axl is in a band called the Boogie Knights. He plays the electric lute.

▶ He loves to cook and works with Chef Éclair, the royal cook – which really bugs Chef Éclair.

▶ Where Axl is from in the Hill Country, nobody has a last name.

"Food now. Lotsa food."

MACY HALBERT

Macy wants to be a knight so badly, it hurts. She worked so hard at Knights' Academy that she came in second in her class, right behind Clay. So on graduation day, why didn't the king give her a shield?

Because King Halbert is her dad, and he doesn't want Macy running around and fighting stuff. He wants her to learn the business side of running the kingdom of Knighton – attending ceremonies and managing villages and stuff like that. Stuff that Macy thinks is the most boring stuff in the world.

But Macy is determined to be a knight – a really good knight – and when monsters attack the kingdom she borrows her mother's shield and jumps into the fray. Thanks to her training and natural fighting skills, she's a formidable foe in the field.

KNIGHT KNOTES

- ► Macy's favourite comic book is *Ned Knightly, Man of Armour!*
- ► Macy is the one knight who doesn't annoy Clay (most of the time) due to her dedication to the Knight's Code.

"I want to be a knight, Dad! It's what I was meant to be."

MERLOK 2.0

With his long staff and tall, pointy hat, Merlok 2.0 looks like what you'd expect a wizard to look like – except that now he can only appear as an orange hologram! Even though he's been digitized, he's still the mentor for the knights.

Technically, Merlok is now the Operating System for The Fortrex, a rolling castle that's the home base of the knights. In his new state, he can help the team like never before. Merlok can send digi-magical NEXO Powers to the knights, customizing their shields and weapons to meet whatever challenge they face.

Just like any form of technology, Merlok has his glitches, and sometimes he just can't get things done the way he wants to. Merlok can get a little cranky sometimes, but he doesn't let it get to him. After all, the knights need him!

KNIGHT KNOTES

▶ Lance once called Merlok "The Wizard of the OS".

▶ Merlok loves to talk about magic, and will do so for hours . . . and hours . . . and hours . . .

▶ Merlok is the only wizard in the realm . . . but was he always?

"'Tis I, Merlok the Magician!"

AVA PRENTIS

Ava is a like a wizard, but not the magical kind. She's a technology whiz – a genius with anything electronic, especially computers. When the power goes out or the system goes down, Ava is always the one to bring everything back up.

Ava is a first-year at the Knights' Academy. While she's busy training to be a knight, she also works with Merlok 2.0 to help him find all the spells lost in the Operating System.

KNIGHT KNOTES

► Everything Ava owns is high-tech – even her shoes.

► Ava isn't impressed with Merlok's magic spells; she prefers her trusty tech.

ROBIN UNDERWOOD

Like Ava, Robin is also a first-year at Knights' Academy, and he can't wait to be a knight! He's super excited about it, in fact. But until he gets his own shield one day, Robin will keep busy doing what he loves to do best: building and fixing things.

Robin's great at designing new armours and weapons. He's eager to help out any knight who needs something repaired. After The Book of Monsters is unleashed, Robin quickly becomes someone who the knights depend on.

KNIGHT KNOTES

► Robin's dad was the maintenance man at the castle.
► Robin has a great work ethic, which impresses Clay. (And it's not easy to impress Clay.)

KING AND QUEEN HALBERT

King Halbert is great at the people side of being a king. He solves disputes fairly, talks to everyone in his kingdom, and is always ready to appear at a royal function. But the warrior side of being a king? That's not his thing.

That's one reason King Halbert doesn't want Macy to become a knight. He wants her to follow in his peaceful footsteps. The other reason? To keep her safe.

Hama Halbert was born into a small village of warriors in the far east, and she can hold her own in any battle. She really hopes that Macy will follow in her warrior footsteps, and she reminds the king that her fighting spirit is what led him to fall in love with her in the first place.

Friendly and down-to-earth, she is beloved by all of the citizens of Knighton.

KNIGHT KNOTES

- ► King Halbert will sometimes express his feelings for his wife with bad (but sweet) poetry.
- ► Queen Halbert is thrilled that her daughter now uses the queen's old shield in battle.

SQUIREBOTS

You can't toss an apple in Knighton without hitting a Squirebot. These little robots are everywhere, and they do just about every job you can think of. Alice Squires is a fast-talking announcer at the jousting tournaments. Dennis is Lance Richmond's personal butler. Chef Éclair is the royal cook – and also a Squirebot.

Other Squirebots are soldiers, counsellors to the king, reporters, trumpeters and mechanics. When Ava needed two target dummies so the knights could show off their stuff in the arena, two Squirebots volunteered for the job. Basically, if there's a task to be done, there's a Squirebot that can do it – and always with a smile!

KNIGHT KNOTES

► The Squirebots that follow celebrities around with cameras are known as the "Squirerazzi".

► Lance has loads of Squirebot servants.

NEXO Powers

Wondering how those awesome NEXO Powers work? Here's the down-low on the download:

1. Merlok is part of the Operating System of the rolling Fortrex. His magic has merged with the computer systems to create a whole new kind of magic: NEXO Power.
2. When they go into battle, the knights take their shields with them.
3. When monsters attack, *zap!* In an instant, Merlok can send digital powers to the knights' shields. The downloaded power is channelled through the knights' armour and into the knights' NEXO Weapons.

Merlok might send different powers each time, depending on what kind of monsters the knights will face.

Check out the back cover for instructions on how to download this first-seen NEXO Power!

Disco Frenzy

Crash the party with explosive disco balls!

The Fortrex

King and Queen Halbert had this rolling castle built as a holiday home – a castle away from their castle. But when Jestro unleashed The Book of Monsters on Knighton, Macy convinced them to turn it into a rolling fortress so the knights could get around the kingdom quickly.

Robin and the Squirebots went to work fitting out the castle to turn it into an impenetrable fortress loaded with weapons. Ava added a holoscreen to the command centre, plugged in Merlok 2.0 at the controls, and downloaded all of the wizard's digital magic. Merlok controls all of The Fortrex's functions.

The finished Fortrex has everything the knights need: sleeping quarters, a weapons armoury, a training area and even an entertainment suite. But with monsters loose on Knighton, the knights won't have much time to enjoy it.

"A complete rolling fortress, ready for battle and spelled with an X. Because having an X in the name makes it cool and high-tech."

Robin

A knight's shield is one of his or her most important possessions. It has to be strong enough to withstand a blow from a sword or a heavy mace. It also bears the knight's family crest, so others can tell if the knight is a friend or foe.

The NEXO Shields are like traditional shields – but so much more. The face of each shield functions as a Wi-Fi interface and digital screen. Merlok can send NEXO Powers to the knights via their shields. All they have to do is hold up their shields to receive the download, and the NEXO Powers transfer from the shields to the knights' armours and weapons.

CLAY'S SHIELD

The emblem on Clay's blue shield is an eagle. This bird of prey is a strong and courageous warrior – just like Clay!

LANCE'S SHIELD

The Richmond family crest is a white horse. Horses are proud and graceful, and white horses are rare. Horses can also be fearless in battle – just like Lance. He may parade around Knighton like a prized pony, but when danger strikes, he bravely defends his kingdom.

AARON'S SHIELD

As soon as Aaron got his shield from King Halbert, he figured out how to use it as a hover shield. He zips around Knighton on his shield, swooping and soaring through the sky. The symbol of his family is a fox and a lightning bolt – which makes sense, because Aaron is as agile as a fox and as fast as lightning.

AXL'S SHIELD

Big, strong Axl is built like a bull, so it's no surprise that the symbol on his shield is a bull's head. Axl is a nice guy with a good heart, but like a bull, don't make him mad or he'll set his horns on you!

MACY'S SHIELD

When Macy graduated from the Knights' Academy, her father refused to give her a shield. Not fair! But Macy's mum intervened, and Queen Halbert gave Macy her own shield, the one she used in her fighting days. It bares the image of a fierce dragon, in honour of her mother's eastern heritage. Ava retrofitted it with Wi-Fi for her so that Macy can use it to receive the Nexo Powers.

NEXO KNIGHTS Weapons

Every knight has a favourite weapon, whether it's a sword, a lance, a bow and arrow, a power axe or a mace. Weapons like these are great for jousting or fighting mortal enemies – but they don't do much against magical monsters. That's where the NEXO Weapons come in.

In a monster fight, Merlok can download NEXO Powers to the knights that will make their weapons especially effective at defeating the monster they're facing. So if Axl is facing an Icy Frost Monster, Merlok can send him a NEXO Power to turn his axe into a giant flame!

CLAY'S SWORD

Clay's weapon is a Single-Handed Claymore Sword, to be exact. It has a cross-hilt (handle) and a long blade that is almost taller than Clay!

Clay is pretty much a sword master. He can hack through practice targets in a matter of seconds. ("Hacking things to bits helps him think," says Aaron.)

LANCE'S LANCE

Yes, Lance's favourite weapon has the same name as him. A lance is a long pole or spear designed to be used by knights riding on horseback. During a joust, Lance can knock opponents off their horses with his trusty lance. During a battle, Lance can swing it to knock down big monsters, or use it like a spear to skewer tiny Globlins made of lava.

AARON'S BLAZER BOW

Aaron is an amazing archer who can hit just about any target with amazing agility and speed. When he goes into "Music Mode", he strums his bow like he's playing an electric guitar, and the arrows fly out, timed to the beat.

AXL'S POWER AXE

Axl's weapon is sharp on both sides, perfect for slicing (which comes in handy when you need to carve some meat), while the flat edge of his axe is just right for pounding and smashing. And Axl's really good at both of those things.

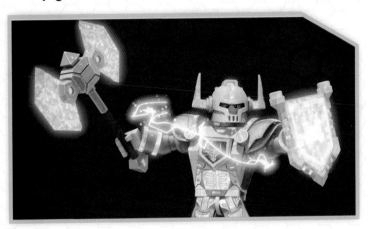

MACY'S POWER MACE

A mace is a weapon with a heavy head on the end, which, like the end of Axl's axe, is also good for pounding and

smashing. Together, Axl and Macy perform the "Whirling Macy". Axl picks up Macy by the feet and spins her around. She uses her mace to "break up that monster pack into a monster mash," as Lance once said.

NEXO KNIGHTS Armour

Every knight needs a metal suit of armour to protect him or her from attacks. The knights have high-tech armour, of course. When the NEXO Power courses through their armour, they get extra strength, skills and protection.

Robin Underwood has a plan to upgrade the knights' armour with different kinds of robotic appendages. Imagine you're in a battle and four monsters come at you at once. Having some extra arms could come in handy!

Knighton was free from monsters for one hundred years – until now. The Book of Monsters is loose, and all it takes is one wave of a magic staff (stolen from Merlok's library) to release the monsters on its pages.

And who's doing all that staff waving? It's Jestro, formerly the king's jester, and now a bad guy. He was a bad jester, but he's pretty good at being bad! And what about those monsters jumping off the pages? Well, each one is more terrifying than the next! What's worse is that the bad guys are hunting down the eleven Books of Dark Magic. Each time they find a new book, The Book of Monsters swallows it whole, and the monsters grow more powerful. And that means the knights are going to be facing some pretty tough challenges.

JESTRO

Jestro wasn't born a bad guy. He started out as King Halbert's court jester – the guy who dresses up in a funny hat and makes everybody laugh. But nobody ever laughed at Jestro's jokes. In fact, they usually threw rotten food at him when he performed.

The sad jester desperately wanted to be good at something. So when The Book of Monsters approached him and suggested he'd make a good bad guy, Jestro decided to give it a try. With The Book of Monsters calling the shots, Jestro is unleashing evil monsters all over Knighton.

Even though he's a villain, Jestro still ends up being funny when he doesn't mean to. Like when he makes up a rhyme to conjure up the monsters:

Nasty, evil monsters, come forth and serve me!
Make the folks around us wet their pants and flee!

KNIGHT KNOTES

▶ Jestro perfected his evil laugh after touching the powerful Book of Monsters.

▶ Jestro travels around in his own moving fortress, The Evil Mobile. It's hauled around by two giant monsters – Burnzie and Sparkks.

"Jestro the Evil! I like the sound of that!"

"I'm not just a book, kid. I'm THE book – The Book of Monsters!"

THE BOOK OF MONSTERS

You know that saying "You can't judge a book by its cover"? Well, it does not apply here. The cover of The Book of Monsters is a scary monster face with glowing, red eyes and a long, lashing tongue – so it gives you a pretty good idea of what's inside.

And what's inside is . . . monsters! More monsters than you can count. But The Book of Monsters has a plan to become even more powerful. Powerful Books of Dark Magic were scattered across the kingdom when Merlok's library exploded. When The Book of Monsters finds one of these books, he can grow more powerful by eating it! And when the book gets more powerful, so do the monsters inside.

When Jestro waves a magic staff over the pages, the incantations keeping the monsters trapped disappear, and they can escape. When the knights defeat a monster, it gets trapped in the book again – until the next time it's conjured up. That means that The Book of Monsters will just keep growing with power – unless Merlok 2.0 and the knights can find a way to stop Jestro.

THE BOOKKEEPER

The Book of Monsters doesn't have any arms or legs, so Jestro conjures up a little monster called the Bookkeeper who carries around The Book of Monsters. It's a pretty thankless job, but the Bookkeeper was born to do it.

THE MAGMA MONSTERS

The Magma Monsters are boiling over with evil, just like magma: a hot, liquid rock that becomes lava when it's churned out by a volcano.

Each monster is evil, and some are more powerful than others. The NEXO Powers that work to destroy one type of monster might not work on another, so Merlok's got to dive into his entire arsenal of digital magic to help the knights.

Jestro can free dozens of these mini monsters at a time with one wave of a wand. They're annoying, but get enough of them together and they can be really dangerous!

GLOBLINS

These small, bouncing fireballs can be launched like cannonballs at The Fortrex.

BLOBLINS

When five or more Globlins
mash together, they form a
Bloblin – bigger, stronger
balls of fire that are harder
to bring down. A Bloblin can
also breathe fireballs.

SCURRIERS

Quicker than Globlins or Bloblins, Scurriers have arms
and legs and can carry stuff as well as race around the
battlefield, menacing their opponents.

MOLTOR

Moltor and his twin brother Flama are total opposites. Flama is a molten mass of liquid lava. Moltor is a massive mound of solid rock. Individually, they're tough opponents. Together, they're doubly dangerous!

LAVARIA

She's stealthy, she's sneaky, so she's the chief spy of the Monster Army. The only thing that gives her away is when others feel her heat!

BEAST MASTER

Powered by The Book of Chaos (one of the Books of Dark Magic), Beast Master is best at wrangling hordes of nasty Globlins and Bloblins. Attached to his hands are two Globlins on chains: one that's happy and crazy, and one that's nasty and crazy.

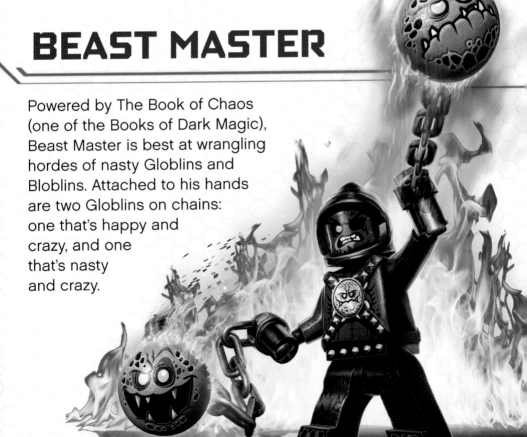

WHIPARELLA

She's got a body like a snake, and she wields two fiery whips, one in each hand. She was created by The Book of Fear, and if her whips touch you, you'll be filled with terror. She can also turn other monsters into terrifying spider-legged creatures that send her opponents screaming.

BURNZIE AND SPARKKS

Burnzie is a horned beast, and Sparkks is a one-eyed warrior. Jestro is always conjuring them up from The Book of Monsters, but the knights are constantly sending them back. They're a pretty scary pair, but they really do make lots of mistakes.

Knighton is a big place, filled with cities, towns, villages, highways and byways. A tour of Knighton could take you exploring old forests, hiking across vast desert, climbing tall mountains or swimming at beautiful beaches. But Knighton is not only famous for its natural beauty. Visitors come from far and wide to see the city's technical marvels – like the awe-inspiring Beam Bridges or the state-of-the-art Joustdome.

KNIGHTONIA

The largest city in the realm is Knightonia, and it's home to King Halbert's castle. In this city, visitors come to watch athletic competitions in the Joustdome, shop at the mall or one of the many markets, go see a movie or dance in a knight club.

For kids who dream of becoming knights, the only place to be is the Knights' Academy, where new knights are trained.

THE LAVA LANDS

Magma Monsters love to hang out in this fiery place filled with active volcanoes, steaming geysers and flaming fire pits.

AUREMVILLE

The western region of Knighton is where Lance's super-rich family lives in an ivory-white castle. Everyone in the region is wealthy – the streets here are literally paved with gold! It's a good thing the Richmonds have an army of Squirebots to protect their riches.

THE HILL COUNTRY

This mountainous region is filled with small villages and mines. Almost everyone is short, leading to the rumour that the hill people were once dwarves. Axl calls this land home, although he is not at all short like his family and friends!

THE DARK WOODS

Just outside the village of Spittoon, the Dark Woods are, well, dark! If you're heading into this spooky forest, make sure to keep an eye out for creepy crawlies. And don't forget to bring a holo-torch!

Behold, Techcalibur!

When The Fortrex rolled out for the very first time, Merlok 2.0 started to glitch just before the NEXO KNIGHTS heroes engaged in a big battle with Jestro and his monsters. With no NEXO Powers, it looked like the knights were in trouble . . . until a digital miracle saved the day.

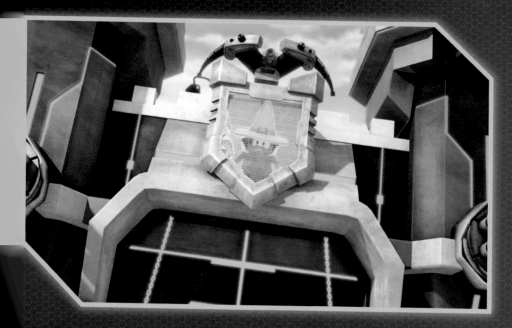

The five knights were just getting used to The Fortrex when Merlok 2.0's holographic image appeared on a pedestal inside the rolling fortress.

"Attention, knights! Jestro is on his way to Waterton!" the wizard announced.

"Waterton! That's ridiculous!" cried Clay Moorington.

"That soggy burg? Who cares?" asked Lance with a yawn. As far as he knew, that town didn't even have a knight club.

Merlok 2.0 glared down at the blond knight. "If Waterton is destroyed, a third of the kingdom would have no water. Nothing to drink. No swimming pools . . . no Jacuzzis."

Lance's eyes got wide. "What? That's ridiculous!" he cried. "There's no time to waste, man! Let's go!"

Over by Waterton, Jestro, the king's former court jester, climbed to the top of a hill overlooking the pretty little town. He was a strange sight, in his colourful jester's uniform and white painted face. But even stranger was the crowd he travelled with.

Beside him, a little red monster held a book with an evil face: The Book of Monsters. Behind them was a small army of Magma Monsters that Jestro had released from the book. Small, round Globlins looked like living balls of fire. Towering over them were two tall monsters. Burnzie had devilish horns and a mouth full of sharp fangs. Sparkks was a one-eyed, muscled beast. They both held wicked-looking weapons.

Jestro smiled. "So quiet. So lovely," he said, looking down at the village. Then he turned to his monsters. "Now burn it to the ground!"

Suddenly, a rumbling filled the air, and the ground underneath Jestro and The Book of Monsters began to shake. The huge Fortrex suddenly appeared, blocking the way to the town.

"What the heck is that?" The Book of Monsters asked.

The drawbridge opened, and Clay roared out on his sword vehicle, a sword-shaped car with two motorcycles attached to the main engine. Big knight Axl and freckle-faced Macy sat in each of the cycles.

Next, Aaron the thrill-seeking knight flew out on his hover shield, and Lance sped out behind him on his mecha steed, a high-tech cycle that looked like a horse.

Clay released Macy's and Axl's cycles, and they zoomed forward through the lines of the monster army. Globlins flew everywhere, and Burnzie and Sparkks fell backwards.

"So what do we do now?" Jestro asked.

"Your invincible army is getting pounded like pizza dough," replied The Book of Monsters. "Get them out of the way of those monster mowers. Onto the roofs!"

Jestro nodded. "To the roofs! To the roofs!" he yelled.

The monsters obeyed, jumping up and out of the way of the cycles. Clay, Axl, Macy and Lance parked their cycles and charged after the monsters, brandishing the weapons. Aaron flew alongside them.

"Time to put our NEXO Powers to use on Jestro's army!"

Clay shouted. Then he and the other knights held up their shields. "Merlok, NEXOOOOO KNIGHT!"

An orange, swirling glow appeared above the knights – and then fizzled out. Jestro did a little dance.

"They've got nothing! Attack!" he cried.

Clay frowned. "No Wi-Fi signal? Really? Looks like we're doing this old-school."

Inside the command centre, Ava Prentis and Robin Underwood were frantically trying every trick they knew to get Merlok 2.0's power back up.

"Glippity, gloppity, goo!" sputtered Merlok 2.0. "Blast! It's not working!"

"You've got to be fully integrated into the rolling castle's systems," said Ava, the tech whiz of the team.

Outside, the knights were fighting back with a move called the "Whirling Macy". Axl swung Macy around by her feet, and her weapon – a power mace –

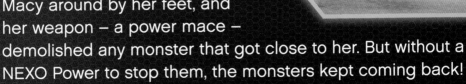

demolished any monster that got close to her. But without a NEXO Power to stop them, the monsters kept coming back!

"We must do something, my child!" Merlok told Ava. "They are in dire n-n-need!"

Ava lifted up a long object that looked like a sword.

"We have to try this," she said. "I call it Techcalibur. It's a flash drive I designed to transfer huge files, like your program. If I can get you into the main Fortrex computers you'll have no trouble uploading your spells. But it's untested. If this doesn't work, you could be . . . lost forever."

Merlok thought. "I understand," he said finally. "But I know you'll work your magic, too. Now, make it so!"

Holding her breath, Ava slipped Techcalibur into the pedestal projecting Merlok 2.0's hologram. The drive sucked in the wizard's image. Ava pulled it out and then inserted it

into a port on the central computer.

There was a sizzling sound . . . and then everything in The Fortrex lit up brightly. Merlok 2.0's hologram appeared back on the pedestal, glowing with power.

"I am Merlok 2.0 DigiMage Supreme!" he announced.

Macy saw the bars on the front of Clay's shield jump from one to five.

"Five bars, Clay!" she said. "We have five bars!"

"Wow! Amazing!" he said.

The knights once again held up their shields. Macy called out triumphantly: "NEXOOOOO KNIGHT!"

Above them, an orange symbol of weapons appeared.

"NEXO Power: Alliance of The Fortrex!" cried Merlok.

Whoosh! The power downloaded into the NEXO Weapons.

Aaron zipped past monsters on his hover shield, firing off glowing arrows. *Bam!* Five monsters defeated in seconds.

Bash! Axl smashed Globlins with the back of his power axe.

Wham! Macy smacked five monsters with her glowing mace, and they all disappeared!

Lance charged through the monster army, his lance pointed at Burnzie.

Pow! Lance got him, and Burnzie was sent back into The Book of Monsters.

"Oh, man. Sorry, boss!" he said.

Whack! Clay swung his sword at Sparkks, sending the monster back into the book next.

With their biggest monsters out, Jestro and The Book of Monsters ran away. The five knights got together and struck a heroic pose.

"Do we have to pose heroically after every battle?" asked Macy.

"Yes," replied Clay. "It's in the battle manual!"

Stop That Book!

It's a race against time as the knights try to find the eleven Books of Dark Magic before The Book of Monsters gobbles them all up. It won't be easy for the knights – they'll have to fight more powerful monsters in every battle, and hope that Merlok 2.0 doesn't glitch out when they need him most.

What will happen if The Book of Monsters succeeds, and eats all eleven evil books? The knights don't know for sure . . . but they *do* know that as long as they stick together, there's no villain they can't defeat!